# Tabby is a Cat Who Likes to Paint

Written &
Illustrated by

## Melissa L. Hillmer

Dedicated to my amazing
family (humans and cats):
thank you for loving
and supporting me
in everything I do.

Published by Orange Hat Publishing 2021
ISBN 9781645382263

Copyrighted © 2021 by Melissa L. Hillmer
All Rights Reserved
Tabby is a Cat Who Likes to Paint
Written & illustrated by Melissa L. Hillmer

For information, please contact:
Orange Hat Publishing
www.orangehatpublishing.com
Waukesha, WI

I am an
*artist.*

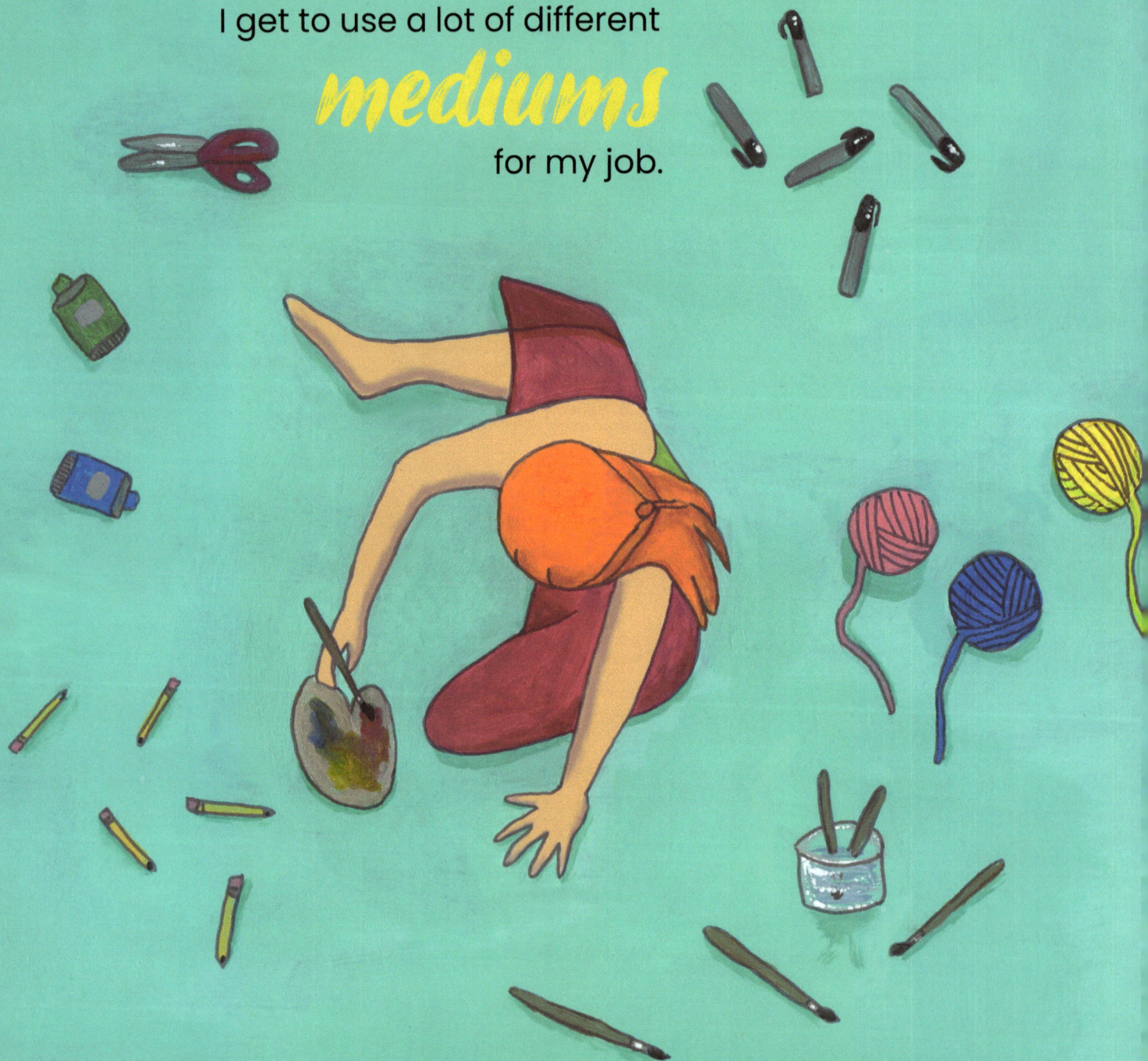

I get to use a lot of different **mediums** for my job.

Some of my favorites are *drawing & painting,*

SEWING & WEAVING,

and collaging & sculpting.

Tabby is my

cat.

She's also my
studio assistant.

Tabby is a cat
who likes to
**paint.**

She helps me build
# canvases
using fabric and wooden
## stretcher bars.

Tabby inspires me with
new ideas for paintings.

She's a great *model.*

Tabby helps me choose the right paintbrush and **palette knife** for each new piece of artwork.

How to
mix
colors

We use the
COLOR
WHEEL
to help us mix
the right colors.

12

Painting can be a little
*messy.*

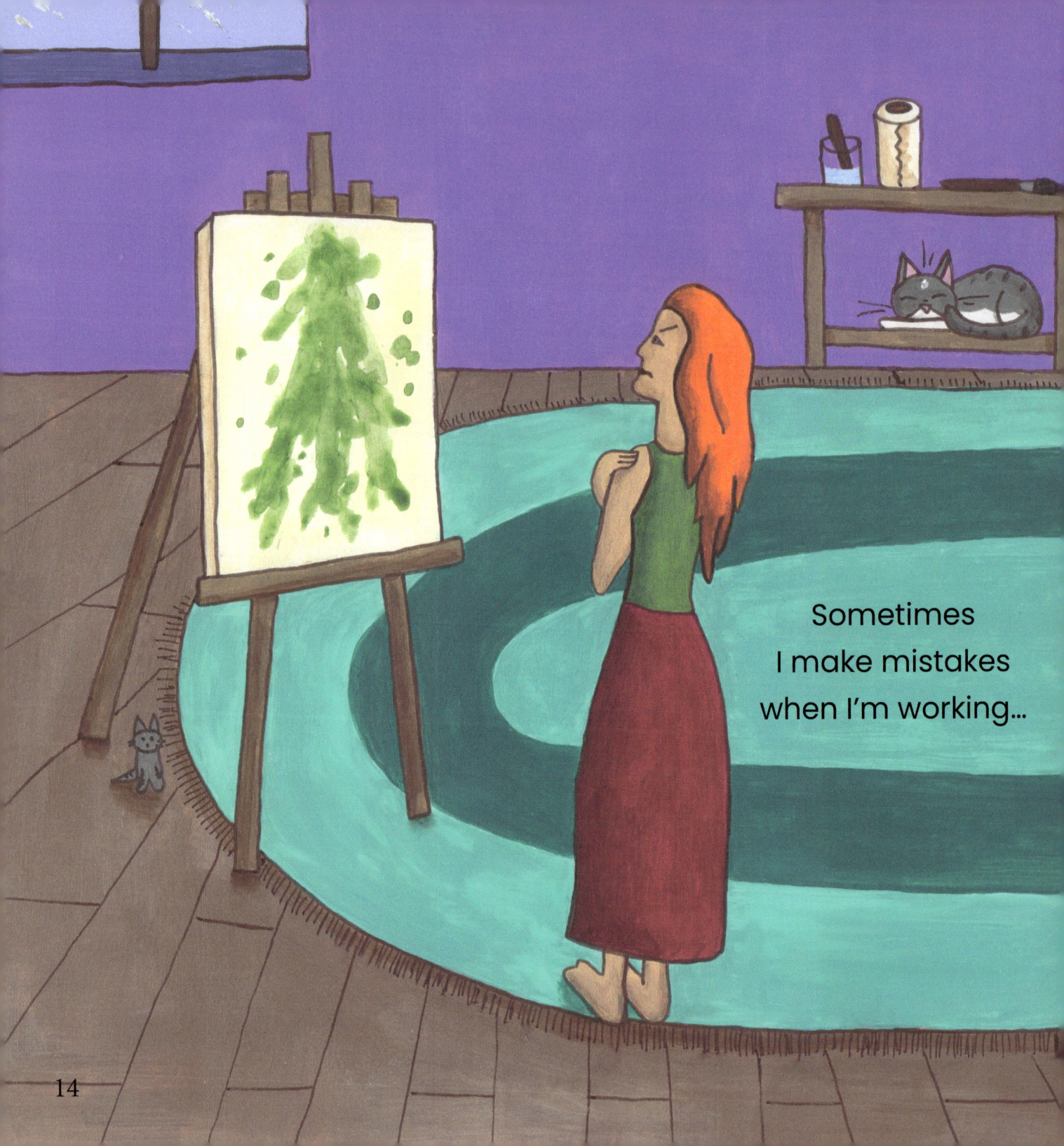

Sometimes
I make mistakes
when I'm working...

14

But Tabby reminds
me that accidents
can turn into beautiful
*masterpieces.*

When we finish a painting,
we invite our friends and
family over to see it.

16

After a long
day of hard
work,

Tabby
helps me
clean up.

17

I am lucky to have
a talented friend like

# Tabby!

# Glossary

## Canvases

Strong, coarse cloth stretched tightly over a wooden frame; used as a surface for paintings

## Collaging

A work of art created through the process of cutting and pasting objects together, such as newspaper or magazines

## COLOR WHEEL

A circle which shows the relationships colors have to one another

## Drawing

A picture made using a pencil, pen, or ink

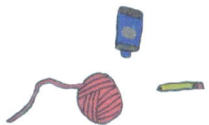

## Mediums

The type of materials an artist uses

# Glossary

## Model

An object or person who poses as a reference for a drawing, painting, or sculpture

## Painting

A picture made using paints (watercolors, acrylics, oils, etc.)

## Palette Knife

A flat-edged utensil that is used to mix paint

## Sculpting

A three-dimensional work of art made using clay, plaster, metal, etc.

# Glossary

### SEWING

A work of art that is made using a needle and thread

### Stretcher Bars

A wooden frame in which canvas fabric is tightly wrapped across to make a stretched canvas

### Studio Assistant

Someone who helps the artist with their duties and artmaking

### WEAVING

A work of art made by entwining two threads together in an "over, under" pattern

Tabby and I have created a lot of artwork and have been on many adventures together.

## Now it's your turn!

Here's how you can draw your own Tabby.

Share your drawings on social media using the hashtag #TabbyisaCat

**I can't wait to see what adventures you and Tabby go on together!**

**1**

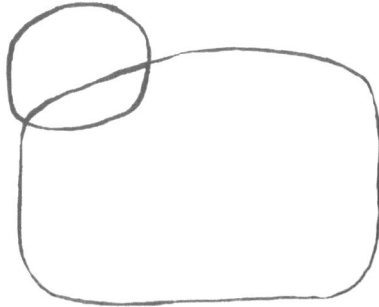

**2**

**3**

**4**

**5**

**6**

# About the Author/Illustrator

Melissa and her cat, Tabby, are from Waukesha, Wisconsin. Melissa became a professional artist and art educator after graduating from the University of Wisconsin–Milwaukee in 2017. She owns a private art school called Otto's Fine Art Academy, where she teaches K-12 art classes and summer camps and leads girls' and boys' scouting events. Melissa loves cats, particularly her best friend Tabby, who inspired her to write and illustrate children's books so that she may spread her love of art and teaching to many.

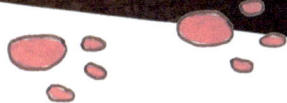

www.ingramcontent.com/pod-product-compliance
Lightning Source LLC
Chambersburg PA
CBHW042112040426
42448CB00002B/243